OLD HAVANA, CUBA

OLD HAVANA, CUBA

Nicolas Sapieha

Photographs by Francesco Venturi and Nicolas Sapieha

Tauris Parke Books, London

Art of Navigation.
Astronomic Navigation.
Theory and Practice.
Whose new measurements for the
declination of the sun, are
reckoned off
Havana's Meridian

*Lazaro Flores, from his seventeenth-century
treatise on the Art of Navigation.*

For Andrés, Regla, Rolando and Alberto – sons and daughters of the
Americas, heirs of Columbus, Bolivar and Juarez – to them, this book is
dedicated.

The author and photographer would like to thank the following for their help in the production of this book: Carlos Rafael Rodriguez, *Vice President of Cuba; His Excellency, the Italian Ambassador,* Carlo Civiletti; Cesare Corti, *Italian Embassy;* Carlos Gomez Owen, *Minister Counsellor Cuban Embassy at Lisbon;* Eusebio Leal Spengler, *Historian, City of Havana and Keeper of Havana's Museum of the City;* Roland Torres Grillo, *Museum of the City of Havana;* Lic. Andrés D. Rofes Maza, *Ministry of Foreign Affairs;* Lic. Adelaida Serviat Peña, *Director of Cultural Affairs, Ministry of Foreign Affairs, Havana;* Lic. Regla Diaz Hernandez, *Ministry of Foreign Affairs, Havana;* Dr Luis Correia Leite, *Lisbon;* Anthony Crombie, *Secretary for Cultural Affairs, British Embassy, Havana;* James Nelson Goodsell, *Christian Science Monitor, Boston;* Sumner Gerard, *Morning Watch, Inc. Fort Lauderdale, Florida;* Alberto Lauro, *Archivist, Museum of the City of Havana;* Arq. Victor Marin, *CNCRM Havana.*

Published by Tauris Parke Books
110 Gloucester Avenue, London NW1 8JA
In association with KEA Publishing Services Ltd., London

Text © 1990 Nicolas Sapieha
Photographs © 1990 Francesco Venturi/KEA Publishing
Services Ltd.

Travel to Landmarks

Series Editor: Judy Spours
Editorial Assistant: Elizabeth Harcourt
Editor: Marilyn Inglis
Designer: David Robinson
Maps by John Hewitt
All photographs by Francesco Venturi and Nicolas Sapieha

British Library Cataloguing in Publication Data

Sapieha, Nicolas
    Old Havana, Cuba. – (Travel to landmarks)
    1. Cuba. Havana. Visitors' guides
    I. Title   II. Series
    917.291230464

    ISBN 1-85043 219-8
    ISBN 1-85043 221-X pbk

Photosetting by Litho Link Ltd., Welshpool, Powys, U.K.
Colour separation by Fabbri, Milan, Italy
Printed by Fabbri, Milan, Italy

FRONTISPIECE Part of the great hall of the Capitolio with its avenue of lamps, marble pillars and vaulted ceiling.

Contents

Introduction

A Cuban monument of great importance, El Templete was built in 1827 to mark the city's founding and the site of its first Mass. Its interior three murals painted by the French artist, Jean Baptiste Vermay, tell the story of the first Mass, the first Town Council meeting and the inauguration of El Templete. Vermay was later founder of Havana's Bellas Artes.

Old Havana is a morning town. It is then, with some imagination and a little knowledge, that the city and its history come alive. From an *azotea* or rooftop, where the washing is hung, where in the early years of the revolution chickens were kept and vegetables grown, where long ago slaves lived, it is from there that day begins. On an early morning Old Havana unfurls like a banner; the ochres, blues, greens and pinks of its buildings sharpen against the vanishing night shadow, while below, still dark, their façades and the streets meld into straight lines. Radiating like the ribs of a great fan, they narrow to a point on the harbour's reach. Like fans carried by Cuban ladies of old to dispel the heat and punctuate polite conversation, so too Havana's streets, lined with arcades, offer refuge from the heat of the day. And with their straight lines, the streets punctuate its urban grid.

As the city of Havana evolved at the end of the sixteenth century, so did the urban grid. A chessboard, its pieces were the buildings that defined the squares, and the emerging city blocks, configured by narrow, rectangular streets. This urban layout, at one time distinctive to Havana, became the blueprint for the colonial cities of the Americas.

One of the greatest acts of creation by one nation, one people, was the urban rectilinear plan brought by Spain to Havana and the other cities it constructed in the New World. Of the many forces which impelled this order was the chaos of European towns and cities at the close of the Middle Ages. This search for order found expression in the creation of Havana's urban grid, and the survival today of this urban complex of Old Havana is not only of note on the island of Cuba but is also of great historical significance within the context of all the Americas.

The architecture that remains in Old Havana continues to offset this extraordinary creation. Within the parameters of what were once its city walls stand some 900 buildings of outstanding historic importance. This precinct of three or more square miles bordering the city's harbour, contains a wealth of wharves, churches, mansions, palaces, simple dwellings and fortresses. These buildings, in the detail of their architecture or design, express an eloquence and a celebration of three centuries of architectural style.

Essentially unchanged for centuries, this collection of buildings is of universal importance to the history of art and architecture – of the more

ABOVE LEFT A moat, although better described as a fosse, surrounds Castillo Real de la Fuerza and separates it from both the Palacio del Segundo Cabo and the Plaza de Armas. Although the fosse had little purpose once the city was constructed behind it, when first built it was essential to the fort's defence.

OPPOSITE The arcade of the Palace of the Captains General runs the full length of the building, its row of columns constructed to define the palace's front plane. Colonnaded façades can be entered easily and offer shelter from Havana's heat and sudden rain.

ABOVE RIGHT The patio of the Palace of the Captains General was only completed in 1862 and in its centre was placed a statue of Christopher Columbus, the work of Giovanni Cucciari, an Italian sculptor.

than 900 buildings of historic importance only 101 date from this century. Some 460 are from the last century, 200 from the eighteenth century, and perhaps most astonishing, 144 date from the sixteenth and seventeenth centuries. Because of this UNESCO in 1982 designated Old Havana a World Heritage Site.

Old Havana is now a construction site. In the past decade the Cuban government has restored some 68 buildings and the work continues. There are few buildings of importance without scaffolding, plaster and cement and the expectation is that this will continue well into the next century. Major renovations are planned for the most important buildings and the others will at least get face-lifts.

Woven into this mêlée of renovation are the simple dwellings and blocks of flats where people continue to live and work despite the reconstruction going on around them. Because many of the buildings within Old Havana remain inhabited, just as they have always been, it retains a vitality created by 400 years of habitation. The city administrators have no intention of moving all of the people from the old quarter, except as a temporary measure. The work is slow because there is little money to move people and there is a lack of temporary housing in other parts of the city, so restoration goes on around the inhabitants.

The concern shown for the heart of Old Havana is recent – during the 1960s and early 1970s, government policy was to persuade people to remain in rural areas to encourage agricultural output and to prevent migration into the city. As a result Havana, like other cities in Cuba, was left as it was. So abandoned were some of Havana's buildings that in a recent storm some 87 collapsed in part or entirely. But that has changed and the restoration of Old Havana has a budget of 6 million pesos a year ($7,800,00 US), some 800 people are employed in the restoration work and funds have come from numerous sources including private individuals, commercial firms, and the governments of other countries.

The driving force behind the restoration has been Havana's city historian, Eusebio Leal Spengler. Just as de la Torre and Tacon, governor and captain general respectively, in the eighteenth and nineteenth centuries, ordered and embellished Havana, so too has Leal this century. Havana's three most magnificent squares provide a framework for the restoration. Plaza de Armas and Plaza de la

OPPOSITE Since early in the seventeenth century, the Plaza de Armas has appeared on Havana city maps. It has undergone several changes, the most notable being the construction of the Palace of the Captains General on the left, and the Palacio de Segundo Cabo on the north side of the square in the late eighteenth century. The square displays many interesting architectural features, such as these arched *vitrales* and wooden slatted shutters called *persianas*.

OVERLEAF, ABOVE LEFT This French engraving illustrates the naval bombardment of Havana and its fortresses by the English forces in 1762. Within two months the city fell to the English.

OVERLEAF, BELOW LEFT It is from here at la Cabaña that the 9 pm cannon is shot every evening. La Cabaña was built between 1763 and 1774, after the English departed.

OVERLEAF, RIGHT A detail from la Casa de Obriapia, showing the decorative band called a *cenefa*. This device, of Italian origin, is found in many houses built between the seventeenth and nineteenth centuries.

OPPOSITE The first of the harbour's forts to be built, Castillo de los Tres Reyes del Morro, was also the first in a series of defensive filters which protected the harbour and its entrance. Today Russian ships rather than Spanish galleons are a familiar sight in the harbour.

OVERLEAF, LEFT Although its shelves are lined with a large variety of ancient apothecary jars, this pharmacy on Calle Obispo specializes in herbal remedies for the treatment of illnesses, real and imagined.

OVERLEAF, RIGHT Atop a rise called Angel Hill, opposite the Presidential Palace, is the church Santo Angel Custodio. Originally built in 1695, it was extensively rebuilt in neo-gothic style in 1846. Note the slender Gothic spires in the background. José Martí was baptized here.

Catedral, along with Plaza Vieja have all undergone major restoration. Two others, Plaza de San Francisco and Plaza del Cristo remain much as they always have been, awaiting the restorer's scaffolding, chisel and brush.

The importance of an urban plan in the development of Old Havana cannot be overstated; Spain's rapid settlement of the New World owes much to the imposition of this urban order. In particular, the Plaza Vieja (or old square) drew people into the city and gave them security, and a pattern of life in an alien environment. Defence, administration and education were the advantages a city offered settlers in a new land and the squares and streets offered order and a sense of place. They also offered a base for further expeditions of discovery and conquest.

Since its foundation Havana was the 'Key to the New World and Rampart of the West Indies'. So decreed the Spanish Crown on 28 May 1624, and so it was for centuries. Certainly the Spanish used the port and its settlement as a staging post and base for operations for all its explorations and eventual conquest of Mexico, Florida and the Bahamas. By the mid-1500s, Havana succeeded Santiago de Cuba as the capital of the country.

The establishment of its urban grid and the city's construction did not all come together at the same time. As Eusebio Leal emphasizes in any conversation on the origins of Havana, the city was founded out of necessity because of the sea. The need for a safe harbour superseded any concern for an urban plan. However, when a plan began to emerge at the beginning of the seventeenth century it was more late Medieval in its origins than those later prescribed by the Spanish Crown.

Specifically it was a plan derived from a treatise written by a fourteenth century Franciscan monk, Exemenic, who wrote at length about model cities and whose many ideas formed the basis of Hispano-American urban plans. He proposed a city constructed of blocks, radiating from a central square, which would evolve into a secondary system of districts and additional squares.

Although Havana reflects this concept, it differs in one important aspect. Exemenic proposed a square with barracks, a *cabildo* and a church; instead Havana made a square for people, for markets and for recreation. Plaza Vieja was built without the presence of church or barracks and in the context of the times a square devoted to commerce, recreation and living was rare. It is for this reason that Plaza Vieja holds

Of these two buildings on Calle Obispo, the one on the left dates from the seventeenth century and the pink one on the right is the Hotel Ambos Mundos, built in this century. It was painted white in the 1960s and a portion of the building has been left that colour in honour of Ernest Hemingway, who kept a room there. His room remains as it was when he left it with little but a plain desk, a chair and a bed.

a unique position in the history of urban planning in the New World. Among the many changes that took place in Spain's urban thinking, the one aspect that was rigidly enforced at home was relaxed in its new possessions: at home, private dwellings were proscribed on public squares; in its colonies, private dwellings were encouraged. This unique source of vitality created the atmosphere of Plaza Vieja.

The Caribbean historian, E.W. Palm, wrote about the urban development of Santa Domingo in terms which could be applied to Havana – saying that whatever the plan or the theory, it all boiled down to a simple European transition from Medieval to Renaissance town planning which was brought to the Americas and applied. By the middle of the seventeenth century, Havana had developed, intentionally or not, along a polinuclear axis which extended from the rudimentary Plaza de Armas to the Plaza de San Francisco and the Plaza Vieja.

Three separate Spanish kings issued ordinances and laws for the construction of new towns. Although the decrees were heeded, in fact many of the settlers had already arrived at the same conclusions as the Crown. The need to control the populace, provision ships and provide a centre for urban activities was as much a concern of the new settlers as it was of the Spanish crown.

Practical or theoretical, as Havana's grid evolved, it set the stage for the construction of buildings and streets – the city that was to come and the history that would unfold.

Most especially, though, it is the street names that record Havana's events – minor events, perhaps that would escape the city's urban records. There is Calle Refugio, where in the nineteenth century a governor and captain general, Mariano Rocafort, took refuge in the house of a mulatto widow during a storm. He remained long after the rain had stopped and the sun had come out. And Calle O'Reilly, not as one might think named after an Irishman, but a Spanish Sub-Inspector, Alejandro O'Reilly who was the first to enter Havana after the British returned the city to the Spanish Crown in 1763.

There is Calle Tejadillo, where once stood the first of the city's houses to have a tile roof. The street was also the site of a famous tavern in the seventeenth century. Calle Lamparilla was the first of the city's streets to have a lamp. Ostensibly lit in memory of blessed souls, a more earthly reason for the lamp may have been the jail on the same street. Calle Amargura or the Street of Bitterness had a cross painted in green

In keeping with some of the other twentieth-century buildings along the Prado, the Hotel Regis is essentially art nouveau with Arabesque flourishes. The alternating articulation of its windows and the brightness of its colours are in sharp contrast to the Ciné Fausto, on the opposite side of the street. Abandoned, as many of the buildings along the Prado were in the late 1960s and early 1970s, the Hotel Regis has been restored and will soon be a hotel again.

Although not a part of Old
Havana, the Malecon leads west
along the seafront from the Castillo
de la Punta to the city's other
districts. This view is from the
opposite side of the harbour
entrance at the Castillo del Morro.
When Jacques de Sores and his
French Corsairs sacked Havana in
1555, he landed on the beach on
the far right of the photograph,
possibly in a spring tide like this
one.

on it and during Holy Week saw processions that followed the Way of the Cross.

A small street, Callejon del Chorro on the corner of what was the Plaza de Cienaga (now Plaza de la Catedral) acted as the spigot at the end of the Zanja Real, the Royal Ditch, which brought the city's water from some 15 kilometres distance. The Calle Obrapia, the Street of Good Works, is named for the donation of Martin Calvo de la Puerta, who on Christmas Eve of 1670 left 105,000 pesos to establish a fund to assist five orphans every year. His house is one of the most notable in Havana and is part of the city's museum.

The Plaza Vieja at the centre of these streets provided the city with a common denominator, a well-spring from which grew a remarkable city, local in its vitality and universal in its layout. For this reason and for the configuration of its architecture UNESCO has declared it to be part of our human patrimony. But to understand Old Havana and to see it clearly, one must look closer at its history – the Spanish, French, English and American influences which shaped its destiny and in turn shaped its style and architecture.

A queue is a good place for neighbours to gossip while waiting for fresh bread at a bakery on Calle Obispo. Although grain now comes from Eastern Europe and the Soviet Union, it once came from Peru and other Spanish possessions; a miscalculation on Spain's part since it soon became easier and cheaper for Cuba to buy grain and other foodstuffs from the Americas than to buy from Spain.

1

Conquistadores and Colonists

Christopher Columbus discovered the island of Cuba sometime around 27 or 28 October 1492. In fact, for a time he was convinced that it belonged to a large body of land – he hoped it was the Indies – and was not an island at all. This uncharted territory became Havana, constructed in a place where no previous town or settlement existed, on a remote bay along the northwestern coast of an underpopulated island. Its discoverers and founders neither grafted a European culture onto the fabric of the existing Indian civilization, as they had in Peru and did later in Mexico, nor did they erect a city on the ruins of one they destroyed, as they had in Cusco and would do later in Mexico City. Eusebio Leal Spengler, Havana's biographer and city historian, explains 'Like the Brazilian city of Sao Salvador de Bahia, Havana was built because of the sea and out of necessity.'

To understand Havana one must view the many events and the powerful forces that were at play during the turn of the fifteenth century in Europe. Three particular events were of significance to the establishment of Havana: Castile had driven the Moors from their last bastion in Andalusia, so that Granada and Seville now belonged to Castile; Columbus in two successful voyages to discover the New World for Spain had established a foothold in Santo Domingo on the island of Hispaniola; and Spain and Portugal signed the Treaty of Tordesillas in 1494 in which they divided the unknown but unfolding New World between them.

Castile, now ruled by the new and powerful Ferdinand II and his wife Isabella I, was ready for a new age and as the fifteenth century dawned it stretched out to the New World, driven by the desire for gold, new shipping routes and the discovery of Central America and Mexico. These three circumstances confirmed Cuba's importance and the strategic location of its port at Havana.

Gold was the catalyst in the jockeying for political power in Santo Domingo, and the search for the precious metal spurred the discovery and conquest of Cuba. Once it was acquired for the Crown, its governor *de facto* sent an expedition to the western part of the island to establish a port and to find gold. The expedition, led by Sabastian de Ocampo, who had been in Columbus's service, came upon a narrow entrance to a large channel which led to a succession of deep water bays. Ocampo noted that he had never seen such a beautiful site. It provided shelter for repairing ships; with good bottom and holding qualities it was also an

excellent place for careenage – laying vessels on their sides to caulk and clean the hulls – general repairs that Ocampo's and all the other ships that followed would require after traversing the coral reef-laden, uncharted waters along what became the Spanish Main. For the shelter and protection the site gave Ocampo and his expedition he named it Puerto Carenas. Ten years later it was renamed San Cristobal de la Habana.

In Havana, on the Plaza de Armas, hanging above the bar in a restaurant called Las Minas, there is an eighteenth-century print which, in spite of being two hundred years after Ocampo, shows precisely why Havana is one of the world's great natural harbours. The imagined view drawn from a point above and outside the harbour shows a series of bays leading inward from the Florida Straits. It is a good example of a bottleneck harbour – narrow at its entrance, 250 yards wide – which opens into a wider and elongated channel for 1500 yards. The channel's western reach curves inward toward another channel, bounded on the opposite bank by a steep headland. Inward from this channel is a series of bays and inlets fed by waters of the Rivers Luyanno and Almedares.

The need for a deep and spacious port would be one of the most important attractions of a natural harbour like Puerto Carenas. With the advent of ships capable of carrying 800 tonnes and standing five storeys high, harbours like that of the city of Havana became imperative. Bearing no similarities to faluccas from Provence equipped with oars, these cumbersome vessels needed room to come about and to manoeuvre within the confines of the harbour.

In the early years of the sixteenth century gold and power were the catalysts for the discoveries and conquests; the conquests were tempered, though, by uncharted waters on the one hand and the lack of secure ports on the other. Ocampo's expedition and discovery of Puerto Carenas was significant on two accounts for it provided a secure port and made possible the reconnoitring of major new shipping routes.

When Havana was founded at Puerto Carenas, it was cast in a climate of tropical weather with all its variables. The weather generally came from the northwest and in late August, September and October, this meant hurricanes. Borne out of the direction of the Leewards and the Windwards, they would strike a path across Cuba and, more often than not, across Havana. Preceded by prescient Caribbean cloudscapes, oppressive heat and stillness, release would come with torrential rain

OPPOSITE An early engraving by Elias Durnford, dating from 1763, of the Church and Convent of San Francisco. The building currently houses a giant refrigerator for chocolate, although the buildings are scheduled for restoration.

PREVIOUS PAGES, FAR LEFT Although this may look insignificant, it was the termination of the Zanja Real, the city's water supply for the better part of three centuries. Water was carried fifteen kilometres from a series of springs to this spigot on the Callejon del Chorro.

PREVIOUS PAGE, ABOVE RIGHT With great advances in seaborne siegecraft at the end of the Middle Ages, harbour fortifications like the Castillo Real de la Fuerza took on immense importance, unwieldy as they were. The moat and drawbridge were part of the defence.

PREVIOUS PAGES, BELOW LEFT This plaque, one of the oldest in Cuba, was erected in memory of Maria Cepero y Nieto, who was accidentally shot while at prayer in the small parish church which existed on this spot before the construction of the Palace of the Captains General. It rests on the wall of the Palace, approximately where Maria fell.

PREVIOUS PAGES, BELOW RIGHT When seen from the Cabaña fortress, Castillo de la Fuerza seems insignificant in size, but at close range its strength and resilience are more than apparent.

ABOVE LEFT A detail of the façade of the Cathedral. Note the high Baroque details.

BELOW LEFT Casa del Conde de Bayona on Cathedral Square has one of the great patios of Old Havana. This interior view is of the patio and staircase.

OVERLEAF, LEFT Unlike the broad patio at the centre of the Palace of the Captains General, the patio of Segundo Cabo is compact and vertically configured with large windows designed more for ventilation than a view. As is true of many buildings of the period, the windows are shuttered with stained glass used for decoration and diffused illumination.

OVERLEAF, RIGHT This cupid rests on the wrought iron canopy that was part of the altar of the parish church which occupied the spot where the Palace of the Captains General now stands. The canopy presently stands in front of the Palace.

and winds of great velocity. Off the back of the winds would come the tides, often causing more damage than the winds. For those at sea or those who lived in the early precarious settlements of Spain's Caribbean possessions, there was precious little protection from powerful winds and tides. Many sought shelter on high ground, while others with enough advance warning tried to escape by taking their ships to sea.

The list of ships lost at sea to hurricanes is long indeed. In one year in the seventeenth century, eight vessels and three galleons on a passage from La Plata to Seville by way of Havana sank off the Matoumbe Keys. Some five hundred people lost their lives.

The weather, however, was not the only hazard of charted and uncharted waters; there was also danger of pirates. Privateers, some more organized than others, furnished with letters of Marque, were authorized by their governments to pillage at will. For the remaining years of the sixteenth century the greatest damage inflicted on the new colony was by French Corsairs. As maps were drawn and routes recorded, attacks against Spanish possessions increased – indeed after its founding, Havana was menaced and pillaged for nearly a century and a half.

While marauders at sea, tropical weather and uncharted waters made discovery and conquest hazardous and difficult, one feature contributed a certain stability to each of Spain's new possessions. As the historian Hugh Thomas points out, the British went to their colonies to work then go home, whereas the Spanish came to work, to prosper and remain.

Typical of those who came to stay was Diego Velázquez de Cuellar. Velázquez sailed with Columbus and on the second voyage to the New World stayed on in Hispaniola, where he prospered. From Hispaniola, Valázquez set sail for Cuba on 15 November 1511, accompanied by three hundred men, among them Hernando Cortés and the Dominican priest Bartoleme de las Casa, who was later to protest to the Crown of the conquerors' cruel torturing and killing of the Indians.

Although it was a short distance across the Windward Passage to Cape Maisi on the Cuban coast, the expedition was pinned down for more than two months establishing a beachhead at Baracoa, Cuba's first European settlement. They met with tremendous resistance from Indians led by a chief named Hatuey. When he was finally caught, just before being burned at the stake he protested that he had no intention

of going to the same heaven as the Spanish. He is reputed to have said 'If torture and murder are the wishes of your God, I cannot be part of that religion and I cannot see myself enjoying heaven with such men who obey the cruel wishes of such a God. Are there any Spaniards in Paradise? ... In which case I have no wish to be seen there myself.' Harsh words, but indicative of the treatment handed out by the Spanish toward the original inhabitants of all its colonies.

With Baracoa in hand Velázquez led his expedition south and westward across the Sierra Maestra cordillera, where in the nineteenth century Cuba's independence movement would find refuge and where in our own time, Castro's revolution would begin. Where the expedition went so went bands of Indians, some forced to mine for gold. Others escaped and returned to ambush advancing Spanish expeditions. However, whole tribes committed suicide rather than be captured and enslaved. The last of the Indians to fight the advancing Sanish was an Indian chief named Guamá and his wife Habaguanex. Accompanied by his 60 brothers, he continued to fight the Spanish for eleven more years. Yet within the space of two decades more than 100,000 Indians were killed. In fact, the Indian population largely disappeared from the island, either through warfare, disease or suicide.

With the establishment in 1514 of Santiago de Cuba as the capital, a political structure began to take shape – the eastern half of Cuba was soon divided into municipalities, each with a town council and elected members who with the governor served as the administrators for the island. But the pressing need for gold, and the need for a secure port further west along the island's south and Caribbean coast led to the establishment of San Cristobal de la Habana on 25 July 1514. It was not a salubrious choice in respect of the land itself, since the site was a humid composite of wet grassland and river delta. It seems that in 1518 or 1519 the town of Havana was moved to Puerto Carenas some sixty miles directly north. This second founding of Havana has been dated as 25 November 1519 by Leal.

On the face of it, moving the port of Havana to a remote bay on the north coast away from Spain's shipping lanes seemed a bold, perhaps risky, decision. But a succession of events and coincidences at the beginning of the century confirmed the wisdom of the choice of site. Perhaps most significant was the discovery of Mexico, and Cortés' landing at Veracruz in 1519. Havana became a significant jumping off

Built on what was later called Barlovento Point, the batters of Del Morro were constructed into the fabric of the point's rocky palisade, as evidenced by this photograph shot sharply from below the walls. Canted and graphic in its articulation, it follows a tradition of military architecture and engineering established by the Milanese at the end of the Medieval and beginning of the Renaissance periods.

LEFT The National Theatre or the Garcia Lorca Theatre, which is heavily embellished and carved, was built in 1915.

ABOVE This detail is taken from an assembly room window at Calle Oficios 211. The book motif is apt for Cuba: literacy was a prime objective of the revolution.

RIGHT This interior of la Casa de Obrapia shows a room off the patio. The patio, planted with hibiscus, lemon and pomegranite trees is surrounded by a gallery constructed of stone and wood.

ABOVE The domed Palacio Presidencial was completed in 1922. From the harbour entrance and the monument to Maximo Gomez there is a five block promenade which ends at the entrance to the Presidential Palace.

RIGHT On top of the dome of the twentieth-century Lonjas del Comercio is a replica of Giambologna's Flying Mercury. While the original is protected in the Bargello in Florence, the copy in Havana is exposed to the elements.

point for all subsequent exploration and conquest of the Americas.

By 1540 the search for gold in Cuba had all but ceased but the port of Havana was now on the main shipping route between Mexico and Spain. It had become destination, harbour and warehouse to Spain and its possessions in the New World. Once an established port of call, the city's function in providing services was more valuable than any gold that might have been found. Its importance remained such for centuries and acquired for Havana finance for the construction of its fine buildings.

A map of Havana drawn in 1691 in colours of ochre and blue, and now held in the Archivos de la Indias at Seville, gives a naive, almost aerial view of the city. Onto this rudimentary urban grid are drawn some of the city's important buildings of the time – the largest of these in the church and next to largest is the *Castillo Real de la Fuerza*. This remained the most important city structure for well over a century. Its presence lent the city security to build and to prosper. In fact the *castillo*, or fort, drawn on the map is the second of two forts built on the same site. The history of these forts characterizes the story of Havana in those first early years of existence.

According to the map, the fort's canted walls run counter to the line of the shore. Havana appears as a fortified island, surrounded by a narrow moat of curving bays. The first of these bays stops just short of the tower on the inner flank of the façade that faces out to the harbour entrance. The second of the bays separates the forts from a rudimentary square. This would later become the elegant *Plaza de Armas* which was constructed in the eighteenth century. The third of the bays describes a gentle curve around the fort's entrance and drawbridge. The fourth and last bay draws a partial ellipse around that portion of the fort's façade which faces the inner harbour.

The map also shows *La Fuerza* to be built of three squat and square towers; a fourth tower, rounded and higher than the others, was erected above the first of the bays on the inner flank of the façade that faces out towards the harbour entrance. It is believed that this tower was constructed under the governorship of Juan Bitrian de Viamonte y Navarra (1630-34). There is an inscription with his name and the cross of Calatravca, the order of which he was a knight, on the taller tower. It is also assumed that he placed the weathervane atop the tower – a graceful figure of a woman called Giraldilla or 'La Habana', the spirit

Beneath the cupola in the Capitolio rests this huge statue which represents the Cuban Republic. The artist has long been forgotten. Note the marble bench on the right hand side which gives some indication of the scale.

of the city. The original figure rests in the collection of the City Museum and a reproduction sits on top of the tower.

The design of the present fort, constructed at the close of the sixteenth century, set Havana on a course of spare and taut architectural style for two centuries. The combination of conchiferous stone and caralliferous limestone used in their construction gave the buildings a visual strength and solidity which dispels that transient quality of the tropics.

The previous fort was commissioned by the Spanish Crown in 1538 when Hernando de Soto, Captain-General of Florida, was appointed Governor of Cuba and given the brief to erect a fort for the defence of Havana. He spent most of his time in Santiago de Cuba, the capital at the time, arguing with the *cabildo*, the islands' administration, to release the money the Crown had allocated for the construction of the fort at Havana. 'Why,' they asked, 'should they give money to secure Havana when Santiago was the islands' capital and its only permanent town. One more pirate or corsair attack' they argued, 'and there would be no port and no Havana to defend.'

The answer of course was that the importance of Havana's harbour made imperative its protection and, as confirmation of its strategic importance, Havana replaced Santiago as the capital of the country in 1553. De Soto secured the funds and hired a contractor, Mateo Aceituno to undertake the fort's construction, although de Soto did not see the completion of the job. He set sail from Espiritu Santo on 12 May 1539, leaving his wife Isabela de Bobadilla as acting governor. He died after having discovered the Mississippi River in what is now Louisiana. Isabela de Bobadilla oversaw the completion of the fort and took up residence in March of 1540 when it was 'finished and ready for habitation, for attack and defence' and waited for her husband's return. It was not until a year and a half later that she learned of de Soto's death and of his bankruptcy. In sorrow she left Havana and returned to Castile.

The hostilities that existed between France and Spain in Europe for the better part of the sixteenth century were played out in the New World as well. Havana suffered various assaults at the hands of French corsairs and eventually the first fort was destroyed in July of 1555 by Jacques de Sores and his two hundred seamen. The city as it appeared on that day in July was a collection of *bohios* or huts constructed of dung and covered with thatch palm fronds woven and tied to the

These nineteenth-century caryatids are found along the Malecon, near the intersection with the Paseo del Prado. This version of the Erechtheum with its four caryatids and entablature is amusing in the circumstances in which it is found.

structure of the roof. The traditional buildings of Cuba's Indians, they served the Spanish as dwellings, taverns, offices and church.

On any given day during the shipping season, Havana's port was filled with ships hailing from Portobelo, Bocas de Chagre, La Vila Rica de Veracruz and Darien, laden with alpaca and gold from Cusco, silver from Bolivia and rare wood from Central America. They would take on fresh fruit, vegetables and meat supplied from smallholdings outside the city. Fresh water was scarce but eventually a waterworks was constructed to bring water close to the harbour. By the middle of the sixteenth century Spain's Atlantic stretched from the Sea of Cadiz to the Isthmus of Panama, from there south a Pacific route went as far as Arica.

It was into this scene that Jacques de Sores came on that day in July; he laid siege to Havana and left it in ashes. The city, surprised by the ferocity of the attack, tried to defend itself but failed and by the next morning de Sores and his men burned what remained of Havana to the ground. Until the second fort was constructed, the remains of the first became a corral for Havana's cattle.

The following year the Spanish Crown set on a course of reconstruction, not only of the port of Havana but also the fort. This more important reconstruction included additional fortifications built of stone, with tiled roofs, singular acts of permanence. It took well over seventeen years to complete amid political wrangles, rising costs, insufficient budgets and various architects. But in July 1579, the Crown announced the completion of the second and final Castillo de la Fuerza.

Following the completion of the Castillo de la Fuerza, two other forts were planned and later constructed at the turn of the seventeenth century: *San Salvador de La Punta* was erected between La Fuerza and the harbour entrance and the *Castillo de los Tres Reyes del Morro* was erected at the entrance of the harbour opposite La Punta. In fact del Moro was built and rebuilt in a variety of versions over the following three centuries, ravaged by invasions, battles and the weather.

Two Milanese architects in the service of the Crown constructed both military forts and also the waterworks for the city of Havana. Fresh water, especially for drinking, was at a premium. With the increasing number of ships and people Havana's need for a fresh water supply within the city and close to the harbour became imperative. The *Zanja Real*, inaugurated in 1592, brought fresh water from springs some fifteen kilometres outside Havana culminating in a spigot on the corner of what was *Plaza de la Cienaga* and is now the *Plaza de la Catedral*. Not only did it furnish water for ships and the town, Zanja Real provided water for irrigating Cuba's cane fields outside the city limits.

Demographic changes in Cuba's population were another indication of the confidence the Crown exuded when the reconstruction of Havana began in 1556. Havana was growing, invigorated by the reconstruction and fuelled by the ever-increasing traffic through its port.

The importance of the harbour to Spain can be illustrated by the numbers of ships which stopped in Havana on their various journeys around the New World taking the spoils of conquest back to Spain. In 1574 alone some 101 ships docked there on their way from Spain to the American colonies and some 115 ships called in on their return voyages. And slaves began to be brought to Havana, to work the tobacco and sugar cane fields and provide the much needed labour for the new agricultural economy. The first large scale shipment of slaves arrived as early as 1524 to work in the goldmines, but by the end of the eighteenth century some 100,000 slaves entered Cuba through Havana alone. Perhaps the most shameful period was that between 1821 and 1831, during the sugar boom, when 600,000 slaves were brought to Cuba.

With its internal economy based on ranching, timber, tobacco and later sugar, Cuba began to prosper. The relative peace after the sacking, combined with its strategic location on the major shipping routes to the New World, guaranteed Havana's survival. However, the Spanish Crown maintained an iron grip on the economy with trade and production restrictions, prohibitive duties and taxes. This of course led to illegal trade to overcome the restrictions. Tobacco in particular was traded illegally and smuggling became widespread because Cuban tobacco was much in demand. By the middle of the seventeenth century nations from France to the Mogul Empire had state tobacco monopolies, reflecting the importance of tobacco as a world commodity.

And although Havana was a port of call for many travellers in the Caribbean, visitors were generally discouraged by the Spanish Crown. It reflected the insularity and insecurity Spain felt throughout the seventeenth and beginning of the eighteenth century in spite of improved relations with France.

During this period, Havana's population grew, and unlike cities in

OPPOSITE Designed in terracotta, the tower of the old Bacardi building and the two other domed buildings – the Capitolio and the Palacio Presidencial – dominate Havana's skyline. Note the little wrought iron bat at the top of the tower.

OVERLEAF This view of the city's skyline from the Cabaña records an enormous change from a view which appears earlier recording the events of 1762 when the British attacked Havana.

British North America which arose to serve the countryside, the population of the countryside in Cuba grew to answer the needs of the cities, most specifically the needs of Havana. In fact eighteenth-century visitors to Cuba remarked that when visiting Cuban planters they stayed in town. There were no great country houses; rather, a planter's social life was in town and he visited his estates only as matter of business. So within the walled city of Havana, the country's life took place and this was particularly reflected in the evolving domestic architecture which spoke of substantial individual wealth.

Although much was built in Havana during the seventeenth century – its urban grid established a network of linear streets of varying lengths – the construction of the city walls took priority. When the three forts were completed at the end of the sixteenth century the most reasonable extension of these were the city walls. Of great expense both in money and labour, it took enormous persuasion to convince the residents to contribute money and slave labour to their construction. The walls were not complete until 1740; even when complete they were not of uniform quality and there was considerable criticism concerning their construction and likely effectiveness. To complete the city's fortifications a chain was drawn across the harbour entrance. First constructed of bronze then later made of logs, it was strung across the mouth of the harbour at night and lifted during the day.

But the walls and the fortifications were not as impregnable as they seemed, for the British attacked and held the city for almost a year, changing the course of Havana's history irrevocably in a very short time. Under the command of three brothers, George, 3rd Earl of Albemarle, Commodore August Keppel and Major General William Keppel, an expedition left Portsmouth in March 1762 for Havana. Its complement was five warships, thirty transport ships which carried 4,000 troops, nineteen supply ships, eight bearing cannon. After surviving severe Atlantic storms, the expedition continued north along the coast of Hispaniola, following the route that Sebastian Ocampo had taken when he sailed to discover the port that later became Havana. Had the British followed the more obvious route, up from Jamaica and through the Yucatan Channel, their attack might not have come as a surprise; whereas Ocampo's route was difficult and attack from this quarter was unexpected. Before crossing the Windward Passage, the British expedition put into Môle Saint Nicolas, just as Ocampo had done, and then sailed toward Havana, through the Bahama Channel, aided in part by the stiff northwesterly flow of the Antilles Current. Then, fifteen miles east of Havana, at the mouth of the Cojimar River, they landed troops. The main fleet sailed westward, effecting a simple decoy which grouped close to where the French Corsairs had landed in 1555. In slow procession, the English marched on Havana, and the Spanish surrendered two months later, when they were down to powder for only five more hours of fire. Under the terms of surrender Albemarle and the British were ceded Havana and the western half of the island.

These early American cars abound in Havana, despite the fact that some are 30 and 40 years old; they are cherished and maintained by their owners with cobbled together parts and replacements. Many of the cars are used on movie sets in period films.

2 Colonial Rule to Revolution

The façade of the Palacio del Segundo Cabo is configured by a colonnade which was constructed at the same time the building was erected.

Once again a European dispute was about to be played out in the Caribbean. Spain, in spite of its economic stagnation, continued to spar with its European trading partners, ruining its European markets. Its former trading partners, rather than seek trade with Spain, went directly to the source of goods, often to Spain's own colonies in the New World, effectively cutting Spain out. A further problem was that Spain's colonial possessions produced more cheaply many of the same goods already produced by Spain – grain in Peru, cloth in Mexico – so that Spain could not sell its own produce to its colonies. And the arrival of new European and North American trading partners in the colonies left Spain in an unfavourable competitive position. But Cuba stood to benefit.

Spain by this time had settled its differences with France, and when Britain sought to drive France from its colonial possessions Spain agreed to help France. Britain in turn declared war on both Spain and France on Boxing Day 1761. The repercussions for Cuba were dramatic: the British laid siege to Havana with a fleet of 44 ships, and 14,000 soldiers and took it two months later. The change for Havana was revolutionary; it became an open port and all trading restrictions were lifted. Havana of that year became what the philosopher Abbé Guillaume Raynal called 'the boulevard of the New World – one of the gayest and most picturesque ports on the shore of equinoctial America'. Suddenly ships from many nations could come and trade, re-provision and re-stock. The city was purveyor of salt beef, garden vegetables and fruit to ships on the homeward journey. It was also dry dock and shipyard; and having built auxiliary vessels for the Cadiz fleet, it was well equipped to service the fleets of other nations. Although it was a military port it was home to sailors, gamblers, criminals of every description all juxtaposed against a formal, creole society.

Now walled, Havana radiated along its grid of three squares, the most imposing of which was the *Plaza de Armas*, and the most commercial the *Plaza Nueva*, now *Plaza Vieja*. Although the cathedral was not yet built, plans for its construction had been drawn up. Instead, the Bishop preached from a hybrid church, partly constructed in the 1580s. There were many imposing religious and private buildings, some constructed of conchiferous and madreporic stone brought from Mexico, with precious woods from Central America. But the city's real building began after the British departure.

The period immediately following the departure of the British was marked by the construction of Havana's most important buildings. With the return of Spanish control in 1763 and the appointment of a new governor – Felipe de Fonsdeviela the Marques de la Torre – construction began of buildings that would not only define the city's dimensions but would also lend it the rigorous architectural harmony that it had lacked. When he came into office, Havana had a population of over 70,000 inhabitants and much of the city was haphazardly put together. Under his direction, warehouses were constructed along the city's wharfs, sidewalks and the first major avenue outside the city walls was constructed. Called then the *Prado*, today as *Paseo de Martí* it marks the outer limit of Old Havana; elegant, with a central esplanade and fine trees, it has undergone a number of changes over the decades.

Among the first acts of the returned Spanish government was to commission an engineer, Reino Silvestre Abarca to construct a fort along the headland and above the entrance to the port's inner harbour – *Castillo de San Carlos de la Cabaña* was completed in 1773 to protect what had been the city's most vulnerable flank. The largest of the island's fortresses, it served as a prison up until the 1950s. After the revolution a military academy was established there. To this day a cannon shot is fired at 9 pm, marking the end of the day and the closing of the city gates, a small ceremony which has been observed since the sixteenth century.

Perhaps de la Torre's most important undertaking was the construction of the *Plaza de Armas*; although it had existed since the very beginnings of the city in a rudimentary form, it had never been given the exact and enclosed dimensions of a city square. In directing its construction de la Torre indicated that he wanted four buildings erected to surround and enclose the plaza – the structures were to include a governor's residence, a building for the postal administration, an infantry barracks, and a building for the customs administration. Only two were eventually built.

The first of these was the *Palacio de los Capitanes Generales*, once the seat of government and residence of the island's governors, then its presidents; it is now the Museum of the City of Havana. Situated on the Plaza de Armas, its construction began 23 January 1773 on a site formerly occupied by the parish church. Its architects were Antonio Fernandez de Trevejo y Zaldivar in collaboration with Pedro Medina,

Map of Old Havana. The boundary of the old city is Ave de las Misiones and Ave Monserrate and Egido, terminating at the railway station. The other side of the city is bounded by the harbour.

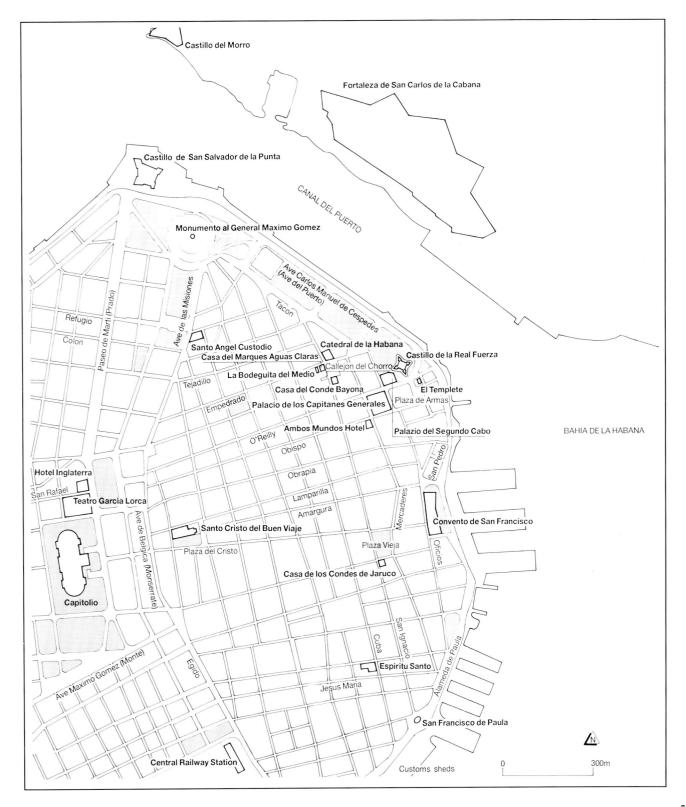

Castillo del Morro

Fortaleza de San Carlos de la Cabana

Castillo de San Salvador de la Punta

CANAL DEL PUERTO

Monumento al General Maximo Gomez

Ave Carlos Manuel de Cespedes
(Ave del Puerto)

Tacon

Refugio

Colon

Santo Angel Custodio

Casa del Marques Aguas Claras

Catedral de la Habana

Castillo de la Real Fuerza

Callejon del Chorro

La Bodeguita del Medio

El Templete

Casa del Conde Bayona

Plaza de Armas

Tejadillo

Empedrado

Palacio de los Capitanes Generales

Ave de las Misiones

Paseo de Marti (Prado)

Ambos Mundos Hotel

Palazio del Segundo Cabo

BAHIA DE LA HABANA

O'Reilly

Obispo

Hotel Inglaterra

Obrapia

San Pedro

San Rafael

Lamparilla

Teatro Garcia Lorca

Amargura

Mercaderes

Santo Cristo del Buen Viaje

Convento de San Francisco

Plaza del Cristo

Plaza Vieja

Oficios

Capitolio

Casa de los Condes de Jaruco

Ave de Belgica (Monserrate)

Cuba

San Ignacio

Espiritu Santo

Alameda de Paula

Ave Maximo Gomez (Monte)

Egido

Jesus Maria

San Francisco de Paula

Central Railway Station

N

Customs sheds

0   300m

OPPOSITE The arcade of the Palace of the Captains General offers shade from the heat of the day and shelter from tropical storms. This small canopy once graced the altar of the parish church which originally stood on this spot.

PREVIOUS PAGES, ABOVE LEFT A view of the Castillo Real de la Fuerza moat and battlements. Note the tiny figure of La Habana on the top of the tower in the background.

PREVIOUS PAGES, BELOW LEFT The Palace of the Captains General had its original entrance on Calle Obispo, but this was later moved to face the square. It has nine arcades supported by ten ionic columns, crowned with the Spanish coat of arms carved in Italian marble.

PREVIOUS PAGES, RIGHT This view of the Palacio del Segundo Cabo is taken from the former American Embassy in Havana. It reveals the roof and indicates where the building is in relation to the Palace of the Captains General.

also a city architect. Although the island's governor took up residence in the palace in 1790, it was not completed until 1834.

Constructed as a square, the Palace is some 80 *varas* in length by 22 *varas* in height (a *vara* is roughly 33 inches). The façade is colonnaded, which not only provides a covered arcade and entrance, but also completes the western extent of the Plaza de Armas. Baroque with many Catalan references in the sobriety of its design elements, the building is constructed around a large central patio.

Almost a continuation of its design is the *Palacio de Sugundo Cabo* which was destined to become the post office, but was earlier the residence of the Vice Captain General. It is a more compact structure than the first Palace with its small vertical patio and windows which let in more air than light. Like the Palace of the Captains-General it has a colonnaded façade and shares the northern extent of Plaza de Armas with the Castillo Real de la Fuerza.

When built these palaces partially enclosed the square. Although the Segundo Cabo and the Fuerza shared its northern side, because they are of different heights and divided by a moat, they do not complete the square but give it an open quality it still retains today. The square itself in its eighteenth-century form was an open planted space, unlike its present form in which there are four gardens each enclosed by delicate wrought iron fences, each planted with a large ceiba tree, a royal palm, rose bushes and a fountain. Outside the four gardens is a continuous stone bench shaded by laurels.

Another of Havana's squares was originally called *Plaza de Cienaga*, but was renamed the *Plaza de la Catedral* when the cathedral was built. Like Plaza de Armas and Plaza Vieja, this was one of the city's most important squares, although it was never designed as such. It is here at the western extent of the square on the corner of Callejon del Chorro that water brought by the Zanja Real terminates. This was the city's water source where ships were supplied. Low-lying, the square is often filled with water during heavy rains or flood tides, but what is most spectacular about the site is its view of the harbour.

Construction of the Cathedral began in 1778 by order of Jose de Tres Palacios, Bishop of Santiago. The brief was to transform and enlarge an existing church, the Oratorio de San Ignacio, the Church of the Jesuits, to create a rectangular space of 34 by 35 metres, configured with three naves and eight chapels built on a marble floor. Although the architect of the structure is unknown, some of the interior work has been documented. The façade, however, is considered to be the work of Pedro Medina and it is Tuscan in the restraint of its design.

Many things seemed to come into focus in that ten year period of the 1770s. The city's first theatre was constructed on the Almeda Intramural de Paula, and on the Plaza Vieja at its intersection with Calle Mercaderes, the city's first cafe opened. Although there had been taverns since the first *bohios* in 1519, coffee only became an important commodity at the beginning of the nineteenth century.

As Cuba's trade with England's North American colonies increased, trade with Spain decreased. The slave trade flourished and sugar began to dominate the economy, particularly after the slave uprising in Haiti in 1791-92. The uprising caused the collapse of that island's premier position as a sugar producer. Many French planters brought their coffee and sugar plantations to Cuba, where they settled and prospered. The market, albeit illegal for rum and molasses, was also lucrative and contributed to Havana's coffers.

During this period Cuba's most beautiful buildings were constructed and it became one of the most elegant cities in the New World. But this growth was based on sugar and the slave trade. During most of this century the issue of slavery and independence dominated the political scene. The enormous social injustice led to a number of uprisings, revolts and outright rebellions throughout the period. Even after slavery was abolished in 1886, peace did not reign, for Spain continued to hold Cuba in an economic stranglehold which ultimately resulted in a war of independence lasting from 1868-78.

After ten years of fighting a general amnesty was granted, but the question of Spanish domination continued to vex the Cubans. Again a second war of independence was launched in 1895 and by this time American involvement in Cuba's economy was substantial. One of Cuba's great revolutionary heros, José Martí founded the Cuban Revolutionary party in response to the continuing repression, but was killed during this second war. Not in vain, because the liberators began to gain ground. The United States government sent the warship Maine to protect US lives and property, but it was mysteriously blown up and the US fleet blockaded Santiago in retaliation. Troops landed and with the help of independence forces caused the Spanish to surrender.

The new century saw the beginnings of independence from Spain but

This interior is of the Palace of the Captains General. It has highly ornate Baroque decoration and furnishings, including a magnificent chandelier and wooden architraves over the doors, windows and mirrors.

Old Havana, Cuba

ABOVE LEFT The Cathedral façade, is a remarkable example of Baroque and Tuscan design; although its architect is unknown and the records of its construction have been lost, it is possible to conjecture that it is a later rather than early Baroque building.

BELOW FAR LEFT A view of Plaza des Armas with its royal palms and *cieba* trees.

BELOW NEAR LEFT A fine turn-of-the-century bathtub and a circular shower were found in the ruins of an old house nearby the Palace of the Captains General. Behind them is the lush planting of the patio of the palace.

further trouble lay ahead. In 1901 the Cuban Constitutional Assembly met to draw up a constitution, but the Platt amendment allowed America to intervene in the internal affairs of the country. Americans flooded Cuba, buying land, sugar mills, factories, railways and began to run the island for their own profit. Cuban presidents came and went amid much corruption.

Dependent on a single market economy, Havana prospered in the years after the First World War when the demand for sugar was so high, but corruption and greed kept much of the country in terrible poverty. Although slavery was abolished in the late 1800s the conditions of the workers in the cane fields were frightful. The lack of educational and medical facilities, the high illiteracy rate and the grinding poverty was contrasted against the enormous greed and corruption of the country's leadership. Machado, on winning a presidential election and in response to protests against repression, set himself up as a dictator. A national strike in 1933 caused him to flee, and the reign of Batista began.

Pressure from the people continued but life remained very hard for the average Cuban. Batista imposed a severe dictatorship on the country in 1952. Finally, Castro began the process which would eventually lead to the overthrow of the government by the revolution. In the early hours of 1 January 1959 Batista fled, Fidel assumed the helm and continues to lead the country to this day.

But this thumbnail sketch of historical events is only the setting for what were dramatic changes for the city of Havana. To understand the evolution of the city we must go back to the beginning of the nineteenth century and to Miguel de Tacon. Three men have shaped the architecture of Havana over the four centuries of its existence – de la Torre, Tacon and in our times Eusebio Leal Spengler. Tacon made order of what Torres began and when work began on the restoration of Old Havana in the 1970s, it was Leal, like Tacon, who made order once again of the chaos of Old Havana.

Miguel de Tacon first became involved in urban planning while governor in the Columbian city of Popayan. When Tacon arrived in Cuba, he surrounded himself with a consulting body of Spanish merchants and set about creating administrative and urban order.

Tacon completed work on the Palace of the Captains General, which Torres had begun. But he also initiated projects of his own, one of

which was a market at the Plaza Vieja. He also began a city drainage
system, introduced street signs, and remodelled the Palace of the
Captains General by changing its lateral and principal entrance from
Calle Obispo to face the Plaza de Armas. He ordered the construction
of a drill ground, once called the *Campo de Marte*, and now called the
Plaza de Fraternidade. He also ordered the construction outside the city
walls of the *Quinta de Molinos* which today is the city's botanic
garden; he widened the Prado; he commissioned one of the city's most
extraordinary buildings, the national theatre on the corner of the Prado
and the Calle San Rafael. Built in 1837 in a Neo-Baroque style by an
Austrian architect, it has numerous statues and a variety of decorative
elements.

But principally it was the building of the *Templete* on the eastern side
of the Plaza de Armas in 1828, which completed the area we know as
Old Havana. Built to commemorate the first mass said on that site in
1519, it contains many paintings illustrating Havana's history.

Unlike other cities in Spain's former possessions, Havana had no pre-
Columbian past. Newly created from nothing, a good number of its
earliest buildings were vernacular. Unlike Lima and Mexico City,
which had been capital cities and had had large sums of money invested
in their buildings and architecture, Havana drew its early style from a
mixed bag of European and American representations.

Throughout the nineteenth century, however, Havana remained very
much a Spanish city. The walls, so long in the building, were taken
down in 1863 and the city began to expand outside the boundaries left
as markers. Houses were constructed of stone around cool inner
courtyards or patios, making them particularly well suited to the
climate. Red tiled roofs reminiscent of Andalusia, and arched windows
like giant fans called *vitrales*, were a dominant feature of the Baroque
façades. In the latter part of the eighteenth century they were covered
with coloured glass and throughout Havana they appear over windows
and doorways refracting the light in a most charming manner. Another
dominant feature was the huge doors which marked the entrance way
into the house and patio. A particularly fine example is the Casa de
Obrapia where a splendid ceremonial entrance leads into a patio of
fountains, orange trees, hibiscus and pomegranites.

Interiors were marked by high, simple white walls with dark wooden
mouldings and the generous use of marble, either from Genoa or

ABOVE A view of the complete façade of the National Theatre. Note the scaffolding around the front tower, which is undergoing restoration.

RIGHT Another view of the National Theatre – a detail of the Moncado Terrace.

The Hotel Inglaterra has a bar and dining room which through good times and bad continue to serve guests. The building boasts fine art-nouveau detailing over the shuttered balcony doors.

Cuba's Isle of Pines. In the salon there were usually rocking chairs, as often as not facing the shuttered windows to catch the breezes and to listen to passers-by; a mirror and perhaps a portrait of an ancestor set off by a chandeler. On a table would be *candela* – a silver or plated dish which held a live coal among the wood ashes for lighting cigars. The dining room, usually next to the entrance, displayed the owners' best plate and china.

The style of life in nineteenth-century Havana was showy and ostentatious. Titles were bought, carriages were extravagant in their design and the tailors and silversmiths did very good business. Ladies, however, were rarely seen on the streets. When they shopped goods were sent to their homes, or they remained in their carriages while goods were brought out by shopkeepers and shown to them in privacy.

Baroque architecture made a late appearance in Havana. When it did appear its constructions were restrained with many decorative elements drawn from Salamanca and Barcelona. Severe as the Palacio del Segundo Cabo appears, there are curved flourishings in the articulations of its entrances; these however are muted and receed into the stonework with only the suggestion of a design.

Writing in 1937, the Havana architect Silvio Acosta said that many of the city's late eighteenth-century and early nineteenth-century buildings were constructed 'through vacillation and last minute changes in design'. The result he said, 'were deformed columns, curious vaultings and capitals that were neither Doric not Attic; although technically wrong, perhaps, they expressed the art of the builder'. But this was true of many Latin American cities: the men who created buildings were not architects but builders who saw a drawing or a plan and copied it, improvising and adding their interpretation as they went along. A case in point stands in San Miguel Allende, a town in Mexico. In the late nineteenth century a parish priest intent on building a new church received a postcard of Notre Dame in Paris, and gave it to his builder with the instructions to build the same thing but smaller. The result is not entirely the same as Notre Dame but it is still there to be seen.

Although no separate faculty of architecture existed in Havana at the turn of the century, a course was offered at the city's academy of art, the Bellas Artes. On 18 September 1912 a group of first year students at the academy were taken to visit the new building constructed for the National Assembly, located at Calle Oficios 211; the teacher assembled

his students in the lobby of the building and gave them a lecture on art and architecture, then with an encompassing gesture said, 'This, students, is architecture'.

Ironically there is no record of who the building's architect was and what its dates were, although it is assumed that it was completed about 1911. At this time, Old Havana was changing fast. A number of new buildings were being constructed amid the old, and though the new buildings were innovative and interesting in their own right, no consideration was taken of the existing style of architecture and a hotch-potch of buildings and styles began to emerge. Calle Oficios 211 represents a new direction in architecture in Havana called missionary architecture, since it endeavoured to break with the past, to find new solutions and yet build within the old city's urban grid. Yet the building's loggia, though covered and ornamented, is not different in feeling from earlier buildings constructed around a patio. There is a curious sense to this building – although it is a blend of neo-classical and art nouveau design and style, it is not European, but has an American quality about it.

Of course there were temptations for turn of the century architects in Havana to forget building within the confines of the old grid since the city was rapidly moving west and new districts were being created, a process that began after the city's walls were taken down in 1863. Garden suburbs, already started in England at the turn of the century, came to Havana in the early part of the century and allowed architects the freedom to build spacious houses along tree-lined avenues in the city's new districts like Vedado.

But architects did continue to build in the old city – a second missionary building was constructed in 1940. Ciné Fausto, situated on the corner of Calle Colon and the Paseo del Prado, won its architect Paturino Parajon a gold medal from the Colegio Nacional de Arquitectos, which had come into being in the late 1920s. Although it was not within what were once Havana's city walls, it was situated on the Prado, the first of the avenues to be built outside the walled city. It is the demarcation between old and new Havana.

Ciné Fausto is a Modernist building and its façade is articulated with design elements that not only emphasize its height, but also its width. The ornament band on the upper portion of the façade harks back to late art deco design. The building is rectangular, filling a corner, and it

OPPOSITE An interior of the Capitolio; radiating from the entrance are halls of great height and decoration, with fabulous marble floors and vaulted ceilings.

PREVIOUS PAGES, LEFT The Indian Maiden Fountain, a nineteenth-century work by Gaggini in white Carrara marble, was placed near what were the old artillery fields and drill ground, which were eventually displaced by the Capitolio and the Parque de Fraternidad.

PREVIOUS PAGE, RIGHT The Capitolio, begun in 1912, is in fact a pastiche of Washington's Capitol and the Congress Building in Buenos Aires. Originally begun as a presidential palace, it was completed in 1929 as a national capital rather than a residence.

These art-nouveau tiles are details from a building at 221 Calle Galiano, which is not inside old Havana but was one of the first of the city's avenue constructed after the Prado and the taking down of the city walls.

OPPOSITE At the Castillo de la Punta and the harbour entrance to Havana stands this monument to Maximo Gomez, the leader of Cuba's independence from Spain. Although Spanish born he allied himself to Antonio Maceo and José Martí in the 1890s in the final war of independence.

OVERLEAF, LEFT Plaster figures of two women articulate an upper storey window of a building facing onto the Castillo de la Punta and del Morro. No records exist of its construction or its architect although it is easy to see that it is art nouveau.

OVERLEAF, RIGHT A view of Havana which includes the dome of the Capitolio.

fits deep into a narrow site. It is the simplicity of its façade that makes it a missionary building.

A third very significant missionary building was constructed for the sugar and rum manufacturer, Bacardi. Delivered in December 1929, it stands on the Avenida de Belgica and the corner of O'Reilly, an elegant example of art deco which fits succinctly into the grid of Old Havana. It is clad in granite from Sweden and a local limestone, and on its upper façade the building and a tower are ornamented in terracotta brought from the United States. Now a government ministry, the building has undergone changes to its interior which alter the original height of each floor. With lowered ceilings, the vertical concept of each of the six floors has been reduced.

The architects of the building were Estevan Rodriguez Castels in partnership with José Menendez Y Menendez, an engineer and one of the students who was taken so many years before to visit the building at Oficios 211. Although Castels has died, Menendez is alive and at ninety years old still maintains his office at the Bacardi building; although it used to be on the sixth floor, he was later delegated a corner room on the ground floor. For the time, he says, their design was an innovative solution, but he points out that Bacardi's other building in Santiago de Cuba, completed in 1958, was equally innovative. Its architect was Mies van der Rohe.

Although the Bacardi building can be appreciated from street level it is best seen from the *azotea* of the Plaza Hotel, now under reconstruction. From here it is possible to see its ornamentation at its best. The sections of tile panelling in terracotta of varying hues on the roof contrast with the sober stone clad structure at street level, providing a counterpoint to the two domed buildings and the statue of Mercury that dominate the city's skyline today.

Just as Calle Oficios 211 and the Fausto need restoration, so, too, does the Bacardi building. In fact, within the complex of the city of Havana there are 2,657 buildings that need reconstruction. The main problem is economic, but it is also a matter of educating people to make use of the buildings which exist instead of building new structures elsewhere in Havana. CNCRM, the government organization in charge of restoration in Old Havana, has recently begun an award programme which cites ministries which have restored or reconstructed the buildings they occupy.

LEFT This little terracotta cupola is decorated with flowers, a dome and an urn on the roofline of a late nineteenth-century office building. Terracotta was a popular material for ornamentation in late nineteenth- and twentieth-century buildings in Havana.

ABOVE A coat of arms displayed prominently on Plaza San Juan de Dios.

LEFT Once the old Hershey railway, this train links Havana from the station at Casablanca across the harbour to the city of Matanzas. The journey is an hour and a half long and passes much of the coastline and scrubland that the English crossed on their way to taking Havana in the summer of 1762.

ABOVE Since Ocampo discovered Puerto Carenas, ships have dominated the city's vistas. It is hard to miss the enormous ship at the end of this little street.

RIGHT This morning passenger ferry connects Havana with Casablanca, an old fishing village just the other side of the harbour.

3   A Closer Look

The patio of the Palace of the Captains General. Note the rather prominent trunk of a royal palm, which has the appearance of fresh concrete. It is now a protected tree in Cuba.

Old Havana invites exploration – whether one examines the old quarter street by street or wanders at random, there will be delights and surprises around every corner. There is hardly a street which does not have scaffolding gracing at least one building. Much is being restored and much remains to be restored, but there are a number of buildings which have been returned to their former glory. Perhaps one of the most charming aspects of a wander through Havana's streets is the interest and enthusiasm of the workers who have undertaken the task of restoration. They are usually more than willing to allow an interested passer-by a peek at the proceedings.

However randomly or methodically one explores, there are a number of streets and buildings which should not be missed. Consultation with the map on page 55 should allow you to find most of those mentioned in this book, but if you plan to visit each of the three main squares and the areas around them you will have seen many fine architectural achievements.

The old quarter is defined by the harbour and by the remains of the old city walls. If you draw a line from La Punta across the park of Maximo Gomez down the Avenue de las Misiones, along Avenue de Monserrate and Egido Street to the Central Railway Station, you will have encircled the old city.

Castillo de la Punta is located at the junction of the Prado and Avenida Malecon and across from Castillo del Morro which lies at the entrance of the harbour channel. Between these two forts was strung the chain which secured the harbour during the seventeenth century. Designed by an Italian engineer, Juan Bautista Antonelli, la Punta and del Morro were complete by 1600 and provided security for the city until the British seized it in 1762. In the years after 1600 several towers were added to la Punta: La Chorrera and San Lazaro were completed by 1647 and two further conical towers and the lighthouse were subsequently added.

The fort was modernized in 1863 and is now occupied by the Navy, though it also contains a small museum. Del Morro, on the opposing headland contains a tavern and affords wonderful views of the city.

From the fort you might wander down Avenida del Puerto (or Avenida Carlos Manual de Céspedes) towards Tacon street. Along the avenue it is possible to see the ships in harbour and many of the wharves and old warehouses built to service and provision the

LEFT La Casa de Obrapia is typical of a planter's dwelling in town. Its severe façade gives way to an ornate entrance leading into a patio around which the house is built. The small detail *(ABOVE)* is of a little statue on the loggia.

ABOVE RIGHT A decorative band of Italian origin, a cenefa, is found in many houses built from the seventeenth to the nineteenth centuries. The craftsmanship and the binding between the plaster and the colour is so successful that few of these cenefas have needed to be restored. The slight fading adds a certain charm to the austerity of the rooms in many of these houses.

BELOW RIGHT This vista of la Plaza Vieja and market painted on tiles in the nineteenth century is found in Casa Obrapia.

Vista de la Plaza vieja ó Mercado Principal de la Habana.

OPPOSITE The interior of an eighteenth-century planter's town house, furnished with heavy carved wooden chairs and chinoiserie screens and other features.

RIGHT The Seminary of San Carlos and San Ambrosio is situated behind the cathedral. Built in the form of an irregular polygon, it was mainly constructed in the second half of the eighteenth century, although many changes have taken place – there are neo-Baroque and neo-Gothic parts as well as sections which were built in this century. This three-tiered gallery is rather odd, as the first two levels are of stone and the third of wood, all of which were constructed at the same time.

These four windows decorate various buildings in Old Havana. The use of multicoloured glass to decorate and articulate the tops of windows and doors is common throughout Cuba.

numerous vessels which plied these waters over the course of four centuries. From here it is possible to walk to Plaza de la Catedral.

Plaza de la Catedral is perhaps the most perfect colonial entity in Old Havana. Certainly the buildings present an harmonious face to the square and the Baroque Cathedral of San Cristobal de la Habana, with its columned and sculptured limestone façade, dominates the square. Commissioned by the Jesuits as early as 1704, the Cathedral in fact was built in stages by unknown craftsmen and finally completely around 1777. Through massive wooden doors it is possible to gain entry to the main body of the church, which is rectangular and divided into three naves separated by columns. The main altar is in the centre of the apse, while each of the side naves has four chapels.

It is believed that the remains of the explorer Christopher Columbus rested in the Cathedral after the Dominican Republic gained its independence from Spain. When Cuba gained its independence, the remains were turned over to the Papal Nuncio for safe keeping and supposedly returned to Seville, although there is some speculation that the genuine remains never left the Dominican Republic. The Cathedral has regular services and it is possible to visit on Saturdays to view the many sculptures and paintings.

To the left as one faces the Cathedral is Callejon de Chorro, there is a plaque on the corner of the building, where a bath house used to be situated. This marks the outlet for the Zanja Real, Havana's first aqueduct. Next to it is the former mansion of the Marquis de Aguas Claras, which is now El Patio Restaurant. Restored in 1963, its delightful courtyard has a fountain around which you can dine. It is also possible to sit on the terrace overlooking the square. The upper floor of the building house artists studios.

Opposite the Cathedral is El Palacio de los Condes de Casa Bayona, the oldest Spanish Colonial building on the square, constructed somewhere around 1720. For a time before the revolution, Havana Club Rum had offices here, as well as a bar for tourists. Now the palace houses the Museum of Colonial Art, with a collection of marvellous stained glass which features in much of Cuban architecture.

On the right hand side is the former house of the Marquesses de Arcos, built in 1741 as a private house, but which in 1825 became the country's first post office. The oldest post box, in the form of a tragic Greek mask, is inset into the wall. Now the house is the home of the

Graphic Arts Experimental Workshop of Havana. Next to it is the Palace of Conde Lombillo. Originally built in 1587 as a tile kiln and residence, it was home first to the wealthy Pedrosa family then the Lombillos. Restored in 1987, it now houses the Education Museum. Opposite these houses on the other side of the square is the nineteenth-century Casa de Banos de la Catedral, an art gallery.

Around the entire square are great columned arches supporting covered walkways or *portales*. Wrought iron balconies and the richly coloured *vitrales* add a Baroque finish to the square.

Between the Cathedral and El Patio you can take a short stroll down Empedrado Street to La Bodeguita del Medio, a small bar-restaurant made famous by Hemingway. Once the coachhouse of the mansion next door, that of the Countess de la Reunion, this small bar now serves some of the best food in Havana. La Bodeguita specializes in Cuban food – simple roast pork, fried plantain, rice with black beans – and, of course, *mojitos*, its most famous cocktail of white rum, soda, lime juice, mint and sugar. Another notable feature of the bar is the thousands of signatures scrawled on all the walls by visitors from all over the world. Although the restaurant is very plain, with simple wooden tables, the food and the ambience have made it famous.

Havana's oldest square, Plaza de Armas (or Arms Square), was laid out around 1519. Now restored, it is filled with flowers, royal palms and marble benches where you can sit and rest from the heat of the afternoon. A statue of one of Cuba's most revered heroes stands in the middle of the square. Carlos Manuel de Céspedes came from a wealthy family of sugar cane growers. He studied law in Barcelona and returned to Cuba to his family business, where he spent a considerable amount of time in jail for his views on Cuban independence.

His most noteworthy act was to free the slaves who worked at his sugar mill in 1868, which helped spark off the rebellion against Spanish rule, leading to the 10 years war of independance. Céspedes was killed in battle against the colonial troops in the Sierra Maestra in 1874, and his memory has been revered by Cubans ever since.

The buildings and offices around the square served as an administrative centre during colonial times; markets were held there and so were evening concerts. This lovely tradition has been revived and on Sunday evenings musical events now take place.

The most important building on the square is the Palacio de los

OPPOSITE This long corridor in Calle Oficios 211 leads to a marvellous stained glass window with a book motif within the decoration.

PREVIOUS PAGES Calle Oficios 211 is one of the surprises encountered in Old Havana. Although no records of its architect or construction exist, it is assumed that it was built around 1911 or 12 by a professor of architecture. The building was first the national assembly, and was then used for a variety of different purposes before its final use today as the seat of local government. Although a blend of neo-classsical and art nouveau design, it has a curious American feel to it.

OVERLEAF, LEFT The decorative moulding in the assembly hall of Calle Oficios 211 is plasterwork at its best.

OVERLEAF, RIGHT Here in Calle Oficios 211 the use of dark wood, stained or natural, for pediments, architraves and pedestals derives from the extensive use of native woods in the colonies.

Old Havana, Cuba

Capitans Generales, Havana's most beautiful eighteenth-century Baroque building. From 1791 to 1898 the Palace was the seat of the Spanish governor generals, and after that the Cuban government sat there; from 1920 until 1967 it served as the City Hall for Havana and is now the Museum of the City of Havana and the office of the city's historian.

Designed by Antonio Fernandez de Trevejos y Zaldivar in the shape of a square, it occupies an entire block bound by Obispo, Mercaderes and O'Reilly streets. The exterior walls are clad in massive blocks of conchiferous rock and the façade of ten ionic columns supports a first floor terrace over a colonnade. Its interior patio holds Cuba's oldest monument, a tablet marking the spot where Doña Maria de Cepero y Nieto was felled by a random shot from a harquebus while at prayer in the chapel which once stood on the spot. Now royal palms stand over a statue of Christopher Columbus and a colonial cannon which used to fire every evening to mark the closing of the city gates.

Although the Palace has had three substantial reconstructions, its design has had a profound influence on the decoration of other houses and buildings in Old Havana. It is possible to see mouldings, cornices, and other architectural details like those on the Palace used to decorate mansions and houses around the city.

Now the Museum of the City of Havana, it contains a large number of exhibits, artifacts, relics, furniture, and domestic items from Cuban history. The original *Giraldilla* now lives in the museum. This six foot bronze weathervane of a woman created by Jeronimo Martin Pinzon between 1630 and 1634 used to sit on top of La Real Fuerza before it was blown down by a hurricane. A replica was made and installed on the castle and the original was stored safely in the museum. The figure is reputed to be Doña Ines de Bobadilla, the wife of Hernando de Soto, who became the first woman governor of Cuba when de Soto went off to conquer Florida in 1539. She waited for him patiently, supposedly staring out to sea, watching for his ship to return. She waited in vain for a year and a half; de Soto died on the banks of the Mississippi River in 1542. La Giraldilla is now a symbol of Havana and her likeness graces the label of Havana Club, one of Cuba's best known rums.

Guarding the portside entrance to Armas Square is Castillo de la Fuerza, Havana's oldest fortress, dating from 1538. It is also the second oldest military construction in the New World. Governor de Soto ordered its construction before he left to meet his destiny on the banks of the Mississippi, leaving his wife and Captain Mateo Aceituno to oversee its construction. The walls, some 20 feet thick and 33 feet high, were to have made it unbreachable. Now it is the Museum of Arts and also houses the offices of UNESCO's building preservation force.

To the right of the Castillo is the eighteenth-century Palacio de Sugundo Cabo, constructed as a headquarters for the Post-Master Generals. It is now the Ministry of Culture.

On the northeast corner of Armas Square, in the shade of a ceiba (or silk-cotton) tree, stands the nineteenth-century neo-classical El Templete, which was built to commemorate the city's founding. The temple also marks the site of the first mass said in Havana, an event recorded in a painting by Jean Baptiste Vermay hung inside. Ceiba trees are supposed to have magic qualities, so the tree in Armas Square is replanted from time to time so that those who commemorate the city's founding on 16 November every year can walk around the tree three times as they make a wish.

Next to El Template is an early nineteenth-century palace built for the Count de Santovenia. After his death the house became the Santa Isabela Hotel for a time. On the ground floor is a colonial-style tavern called the Meson de la Flota, and the rest of the building is being reconverted into an urban inn, restoring its colonial features in keeping with the rest of the square.

Leading off Armas Square are some of the most interesting streets historically and architecturally. Obispo Street running east/west beginning at Armas, terminates at the Floridita Bar – another Hemingway haunt. On the corner of Obispo near Armas Square is the site of Havana's first girls school, San Francisco de Sales, founded in 1699 and open until 1925. There are also a series of restored commercial buildings overlooking the square, Casa del Cafe con Leche, Las Minas Bar-Restaurant, La Tinaja, Casa de la Natilla, and on Mercaderas, the Santa Catalina French Pharmacy, El Herbalorio, Casa de la Infusions, and La Botica, to name a few. These shops have been restored to their nineteenth-century glory and it is possible to browse through many of them. Obispo itself is clearly a colonial street, where cobbled road surfaces, gas lamps, and old wrought iron shop signs help capture the feeling of a bygone age. The corner spurs on buildings

The bar of the Inglaterra Hotel holds an art nouveau statue surrounded by wonderfully colourful period tiles.

When the dome of the Palacio Presidencial is viewed from afar – from the azotea of the old Plaza Hotel – its two-toned caramel terracotta revetment sits above a wide wedding cake block of a building. Whatever one makes of the Presidential Palace, it dominates the skyline. What redeems the building is the permanent exhibition of documents and paraphenalia of Cuba's revolution in 1959.

designed to protect the edges of houses from carriage wheels can still be clearly seen. Close attention to details like door handles, latches, knockers and railings have all contributed to the colonial charms of these buildings.

The famous *vitrales*, windows in half circles over doors and shuttered windows, made of richly coloured glass, are still there. *Lucetas* are square or rectangular versions of this feature. Another distinctive feature of the older houses on many streets are the doors. Main doors tend to be large enough to admit carriages, and are therefore very grand and very heavy, not the sort of door to open numerous times a day. Smaller doors were inset into the grand doors and sometimes very tiny hatches or *postigos*, at head height were set into the main doors to function as peep-holes, out of which one might lean and gossip.

Down Obispo street at Mercaderas is the Ambos Mundos Hotel where Hemingway stayed during his early years in Havana. Cubans have enormous respect for the writer and have preserved his room in the hotel as a museum. They have also preserved his house and garden in the suburbs, keeping it exactly the way he left it. All the rooms in the hotel but Hemingway's are used by teachers who come to Havana from all over the country to attend seminars and meetings.

Another interesting street worthy of exploration is Calle Oficios, where one can find the Automobile Museum, the Numismatic Museum, Arabian House and a Cigar Salon, all of them housed in lovely restored colonial buildings.

Some five blocks down San Ignacio Street lies Plaza Vieja. After Plaza de Armas was taken over as a military and troop drill parade, Vieja became the focus of commercial and social life in old Havana. In order to provide a place where people of the city could 'run bells and hold celebrations', assessors of 'science and conscience' were named to draw up a plan for building a square on the site of the former customs office. These measures, taken in the sixteenth century, resulted in the construction of what we now call Plaza Vieja, Havana's first urban planning effort. It was from the very start a marketplace and a centre for public events and celebrations. Its residents were members of the ruling class, including tradesmen and army and navy officers. They built their mansions with huge portals and tall columns that supported high ceilings, balconies and arched stained glass windows.

The most luxurious building there now is the mansion of Count de

Jaruco, which features a vast entrance door topped by an impressive coat of arms carved on the façade and stained glass arches covering the entire front of the second story. The entrance hall opens into a large patio framed by the high, overhanging loggias of the upper floor, where the family lived in spacious rooms with marble floors, carved wooden panels and precious stained-glass windows. This mansion, the first to be restored on the square is now the home of Fondo de Benes Culurales (Foundation for Cultural Assets). Its rooms display permanent collections of colonial furniture and paintings and are used as offices, an art gallery and a boutique.

The streets off Plaza Vieja are of great interest. On Cuba and Jesus Maria is the oldest church in Cuba, Espiritu Santo, built in 1632. It was extensively restored in 1987 and has now reopened for services. In Egido Street is a small memorial at the birthplace of José Martí, another great Cuban hero. Poet and revolutionary, he served months in prison for his part in the 1868 uprising and was killed in the 1895 revolution.

At the end of Cuba Street just west of the ruins of San Francisco de Paula Church and Square, is the Alameda de Paula – Havana's first promenade of marble and iron street lamps. It has been overwhelmed by the warehouses, stores and bars of the waterfront. During the colonial period this was a busy commercial centre, but is now very quiet except for the Fountain of the Lions which stands in front of the San Francisco Convent built in 1584. The rear of the church backs onto Plaza Vieja.

Plaza del Cristo is another lovely little square adjacent to Santo Cristo del Buen Viaje. The church dates from 1693 and has impressive towers, a tiled roof and cross-beamed ceiling. If you walk down Monserrate, which follows the line of the ancient city walls towards the sea, you will come to El Floridita Restaurant, one of Havana's best and most expensive seafood restaurants. Nearby you will find the early palace of the Archbishop on Habana Street, and the Church of St Angel Custodio with its dozen spectacular gothic spires. The church has undergone many additions and transformations over the years, but in 1986 was completely restored. A walk back towards the sea finds one back at Real Fuerza, behind which is the former Presidential Palace and now the Museum of the Revolution.

Perhaps the last major area to explore should be the Prado, which provides a boundary outside the original walls of Old Havana. Now

Flanking the entrance stair to the Capitolio is this neo-classical figure representing 'Trabajo' or Work, by the Italian sculptor, Angelo Zanelli.

called Paseo de Martí, it is a popular promenade for the inhabitants of the city. On the Prado is the neo-classical Aldama Palace, one of Havana's most important nineteenth-century mansions. It was sacked during the 1868 War of Independence and for years after that the mansion was used as storerooms and offices. It has now been restored to its former glory and is the headquarters for the Institute of the History of the Communist Movement and the Socialist Revolution.

The most prominent building on the Prado is the Capitolio, which is a pastiche of the Capitol in Washington. Built in 1929, the cupola is 310 feet high and the front of the building is some 682 feet high. The interior is almost entirely covered in marble. The building now houses the Academy of Sciences and the Natural History Museum.

The Great Theatre, sometimes called the Garcia Lorca Theatre is also on the Prado. Completed in 1837, it continues to serve as a theatre. Next to it is Havana's oldest operating hotel, the Inglaterra, which has been in business since 1880.

Ciné Fausto, constructed of cement and stone, has an entrance of three metres in width which leads into a lobby, then the theatre proper which has seating for 750 in the stalls and another 800 in the two upper balconies. Although designed primarily as a movie theatre, today it is used for a variety of purposes.

4

Living with the past, looking to the future

OPPOSITE Restoration work goes on slowly in Old Havana because money and conditions do not allow unrestrained progress. As a result scaffolding and piles of dirt and building materials clutter the streets, as here in Plaza Vieja.

OVERLEAF, LEFT Built in 1635 for the Poor Clares, the Santa Clara convent became the city slaughter house and today houses CNCRM, the planning office for the restoration of Old Havana. It also houses a laboratory devoted to the restoration of antiquities, one of the most sophisticated in the Caribbean. This has been funded by the United Nations Development Fund. The picture shown is a detail of the central patio.

OVERLEAF, RIGHT This view along the eastern shore of the harbour shows the terrain, and in the foreground the Cabaña fortress which was constructed after the English seized Havana, shown *(BELOW RIGHT)* close up looking out over the harbour.

Havana is a city of some two million people, a rich melting pot of ethnic combinations; Spanish and Indian, Spanish and black, crowded together in a limited amount of space. Perhaps nowhere is this limitation felt more strongly than in Old Havana, with 110,000 people living in a four-hundred-year-old collection of architectural history – some would say architectural ruin. The density of population (roughly 170 people per acre) is only one of the problems facing Havana and its citizens; up until very recently the old city was literally crumbling around its residents.

Some of the neglect has been understandable. After the revolution in 1959, the priority of Castro's government was to educate and provide decent medical care for Cubans, particularly the rural poor, upon whom the country so heavily depended. In fairness, they have succeeded; the literacy rate is very high by world standards and the medical health system is enviable, with infant mortality rates lower than most developing nations. In Havana, the immediate necessity was to provide decent housing for the people living in the peripheral slums. To accomplish this, new housing was erected outside the city at vast expense, leaving little money for the upkeep of the old residential districts. However, the effects of neglect, overcrowding, antiquity, sea salt and tropical storms were causing this fine old quarter to crumble to the ground.

The Cuban government has now embarked on a plan for urban renewal with the help of UNESCO. In recognition of Old Havana's architectural and historical worth, UNESCO, in 1982 declared the old quarter a World Heritage Site. This designation covers the entire area within the former city walls, certain equally important areas just outside the wall, such as the Paseo Promenade and some of the buildings bordering it, as well as the entire system of ancient fortifications.

The task is formidable. There are over 900 buildings of historical worth from the sixteenth century to this. Of these 68 have been completely restored with dazzling effects, providing a fleeting glimpse of the beauty that once was, and with perseverance, will be again. Although the restoration work goes on constantly now, money is always short. But Eusebio Leal Spengler, the city's historian and driving force behind the restoration, refuses to give up – with little money, enormous energy and great goodwill on the part of the people who live in Old Havana, the restorers have accomplished amazing feats.

Old Havana, Cuba

While extraordinary buildings like Calle Oficios 211, which represents this century's architecture, are in urgent need of repair, others such as the seventeenth-century Convent of San Francisco, needs reconstruction for the third time since it was first built in 1672. Once a hospital and a convent, it was destroyed by a hurricane in 1746 then rebuilt shortly thereafter, only to have its dome and its east façade destroyed in another hurricane in 1844.

Although it had been closed for many years, it was bought by Ferrocariles Unidos, an English railway company in 1907. It escaped complete demolition in 1937 when the mayor of Havana interceded and allowed only the hospital to be demolished. In 1946 it was restored and today it houses the government catering facility. Again there are plans to restore the building and the Spanish government has offered to pay for the reconstruction of its dome and its harbour façade which was destroyed in 1844.

In Old Havana there are many buildings like this, and although the restoration process is slow, the work that is carried out is done with great care. Few of the city's blocks are entirely restored and so each building has to be seen for itself. As each has been restored, it has either been returned to its residents or turned into a museum. Of these, Casa de Obrapia is one of the most remarkable, revealing not only how a house of this kind was in the seventeenth century but also recording the changes that have taken place in private houses since that time. Across the street is another house, which now holds a museum of African Art – some artefacts were donated by other countries, some come from the private collection of Fidel Castro and, most significantly, the museum now contains the collection of Afro-Cuban art and artifacts of Fernando Ortiz, Cuba's great anthropologist who actually lived there earlier in this century.

Although of less immediate interest than the other squares, Plaza Vieja provides a record of how people lived over the years. Mainly residential, it cannot boast of museums, old shops or the graceful architecture of the other great squares, but it does display Havana's architecture as it grew and changed in four hundred years.

A polygon in shape, Plaza Vieja's central precinct is raised to accommodate a parking garage which was constructed in the early 1950s. Although difficult to remove, it is one of a list of changes to the square which UNESCO proposed. They also suggested closing the

OPPOSITE The interior of Las Minas Restaurant – note the multicoloured vitrales, reflecting their vibrant colours on the floor.

PREVIOUS PAGES, LEFT This art deco plaque illustrating 'Fortune' is again on the Bacardi Building.

PREVIOUS PAGES, RIGHT Las Minas Restaurant occupies the ground floor of the Casa de Obispo y Oficios in Plaza de Armas, currently under restoration.

OVERLEAF, ABOVE A view of the harbour, showing the curve of the Malecon.

OVERLEAF, BELOW Cigars are an important export product for Cuba. This one is being smoked in front of the Hotel Ambos Mondos, where Hemingway lived in the 1930s.

square to traffic, and restoration of its balconies, wrought iron and tiled roofs.

One of the curious aspects of the Plaza Vieja is its acoustics. Because they are so good, the Cuban government has initiated a series of concerts in the square; during a recent concert, at a lull in the performance, a neighbour on one side of the square called to a friend on the other – 'Caridad', she began in a loud voice that echoed throughout the square.

Walking Old Havana's streets one is confronted with a crowd of impressions. But it is on the other side of the harbour, at the Castillo del Morro, where you sense Havana's past; her debt to the sea for her existence seems clearer among the cannon, the palisades and the fortress which guard the harbour.

On a Saturday afternoon inbetween rain showers, under the statue of Columbus in the patio of the Palace of the Captains General, there was a concert of Afro-Cuban music. The singer was Merceditas Valdez, long a friend and collaborator of Fernando Ortiz, and one of Cuba's great musicians. As the rain began again, she continued to sing, dressed in white with no umbrella, and as she moved with the rhythm so did the umbrellas of the audience, all under the gaze of Columbus. Although the music and the audience might have been strange to him, these people are indeed his children. Out of the extraordinary land he described on his discovery of Cuba, these people have created a home.

Out of all its cultural roots, the architecture of Old Havana speaks of Spain, but it also speaks of the Americas, of Cuba and of this city. Just as the buildings inherit and interpret an Andalusian tradition, they also carry a separate cultural identity, making their existence and their survival as important as a fight for independence. They are the increments of change, recorders of history and a precious part of Old Havana's legacy to the world.

Old Havana, Cuba

Travellers' Information

Planning the trip

When to Go
For sun, warmth and beaches, the best and dryest time to go to Havana is from November to May, but the most beautiful time to go is during the rainy season from May to November. In spite of the warmth and the rain, it is preferable since Havana is crowded in winter, especially with Canadians. Don't let the thought of the rain deter you; although it is torrential at that time of year it lasts no more than two hours during the afternoon.

Travel documents
Citizens of Denmark, France, Italy, Norway, Sweden, Switzerland, Liechtenstein, Yugoslavia and most Eastern European countries need only a valid passport. A visa is required for Austrians, Canadians, and British subjects. A travel ban is in effect for US tourists with exemptions made for journalists, academics and professionals doing research with an established interest in Cuba. Also exempt are those with family in Cuba or those invited with 'all land expenses' paid. US travellers to Cuba can arrange their visas through the Cuban interests section, Czechoslovakian Embassy, Washington DC, which costs $5.00 US. Travellers coming from infected areas must carry vaccination certificates against cholera and yellow fever.

Costs
The monetary unit is the peso with an exchange of roughly $1.00 US to .90 peso. There are heavy penalties for those caught changing money on the black market. Denominations of 1,5,10,20 peso notes are current and there are coins of 1,5,20 and 40 centavos. Do not change large amounts of currency into Cuban pesos since most hotels, restaurants, and tourist taxis accept, in fact prefer, either US or Canadian dollars. These can be expensive; although essentials in Cuba are relatively cheap, all non-essentials and anything imported is expensive.

Health
Sanitary reforms have transformed Cuba into a healthy country, though it is advisable not to drink the tap water. Bottled and mineral waters are recommended and easily available. Medical service is free to all but prescription drugs must be purchased for nominal sums.

Dress
Generally informal; summer calls from the very lightest clothing. Cuban men wear a *guayabera*, a light pleated shirt worn outside the trousers. Men should not wear shorts except on or near the beach and trousers are fine for women if preferred.

Organized Tours
Most European countries have a Cuban tourist office and in Canada there are offices in both Montreal and Toronto. On arrival in Havana, tours can be arranged through your hotel or directly through Cubatur, Calle 23, No 156 e/N y o, Havana 4, Tel. 32-4521, Telex 511336 or through Cubanacan S.A., Calle 146 e/11 y 13 Playa RPTO Siboney, Apartado 16046, Havana, Telex 511315 Nacan Cu. UNITOURS Canada run tours for all nationalities.

Getting to Havana
Soviet, Cuban, Czechoslovak and East German airlines have direct flights from East Berlin, Frankfurt, Moscow, Prague and Rabat.

Cubana de Aviacion and Iberia operate a twice weekly service to Madrid, Vlasa operates a service from Caracas, and there is a regular service between Havana and Mexico City provided by both Mexican and Cuban airlines. Cuban and Canadian airlines also run a regular service from Montreal and Toronto.

Departing from Europe, the most direct service is offered by Cubana and Iberia out of Madrid.

Car Rental and Taxis
Though Havana has plenty of taxis and buses, cars can be rented, arranged either through your tour company or through your hotel. There are two kind of taxis in Havana: tourist taxis which operate from hotels whose fares must be paid in hard currency, usually US dollars, and ordinary taxis which accept pesos. These taxis may be reluctant to carry you since they are not designated to carry tourists.

Where to stay and eat

Hotels
Havana's hotels range from the Habana Libre, once the Hilton and the largest of the city's hotels to the Valencia, a new 12 bedroom hotel which has just opened. It appears to be a comfortable and quiet place to stay. The British Embassy puts its visitors in the Victoria which has an excellent restaurant. Although far from Old Havana, in Vedado, the Presidente has a good restaurant and has just been restored. The classic Havana hotel is the Nacional which is currently being restored and although it is open expects to be only partially occupied until 1991.

Where to eat
There are many restaurants now open in Havana. The most famous tourist restaurant which serves Cuban food at its best is the Bodeguita del Medio where Hemingway drank his *mojitos* – Havana club rum and soda poured over a base of lime juice, crushed mint and sugar, decorated with a sprig of mint.

However there are others places to eat and one particularly good spot is the Divina Pastora below the Castillo del Morro. If you go up to the San Carlos de la Cabana Fortress for the nine o'clock cannon, take a five minute taxi ride back down to this excellent restaurant which specializes in fish.

At lunch time, restaurants in Old Havana are crowded. Good food can be had at Las Minas Restaurant opposite the Palace of the Captains General. But for a sandwich, the restaurant and bar below the Castillio del Morro is uncrowded, good and simple. It is called the Bateria del Sol. There is also a restaurant at the same location called the Doze Apostoles, which serves good Cuban fare.

Nightlife
Ask your hotel tourist office about nightlife. The Tropicana is functioning again, and there are numerous small clubs.

General Information

Information
General tourist information can be had from your hotel. Do ask for maps. In the bigger hotels, there are Intur shops which have book sections where you will find books on Havana and Cuba. The Abel Santamaria International Bookstore is an excellent bookshop, which stocks a wide selection of books in foreign languages, published mostly by Cuban and Soviet publishers, although there are some from Spanish and Latin American publishers as well. It is at the corner of Monte and Cardenas Street near the Prado. There is also an excellent shop at the Palace of the Captains General.

Time Zones
Cuba is on Eastern Standard Time, daylight saving in the summer so when it is 12 noon in Havana it is 6 pm in London.

Laws and Regulations
Like any place, you should carry your passport and if not then a photocopy of it or some other form of identification.

Access to Museums and Sites
Access is free to all of Havana's museums.

Shopping
There is not a great deal to buy in Havana except of course cigars and rum. There are a number of speciality shops selling cigars, either in quantity or a few at a time. If cigars are offered to you on the street by the box, it is best not to buy them, since you cannot be guaranteed of their freshness, and if you cannot show a receipt for their purchase at the airport you may be questioned.

Shops at all the big hotels have goods for sale. Everything has to be paid for in dollars.

Laundry
Laundry is best done in your hotel where it is always fast and well done.

Photography
Photos can be taken most everywhere. Bear in mind that Cuba is bright from sunrise on, so slower films give

better results. A haze or ultraviolet filter is a good idea given Havana's seaside location.

Electric current
Electric current is generally 120 volts, but ask if you aren't sure. Certainly in any of Havana's hotels electricity is standard.

Telephone and Telex
You can send telexes, faxes and make phone calls from your hotel, but remember that calls from Cuba are expensive.

National Holidays
January 1st the Day of National Liberation marking the triumph of the Revolution.
May 1 is of course May Day
July 26 the Day of National Rebellion
October 10 Declaration of War of Independence against Spain

Canada
Calle 30 No 518 esq. a 7ma Ave.
Miramar
Tel: 2-6421
        29-3393
        29-3892

France
Calle 14 No 312 / 3ra y 5ta
Miramar
Tel: 29-6048
        29-6143
        32-8021

Great Britain
Edificio Bolivar
Carcel Nos 101 & 103
Central Havana
Tel: 61-5681
        61-7527

Spain
Carcel No 51 esq a Zulueta
Central Havana
Tel: 6-4741
        6-9687

Further Reading

Cuba or the Pursuit of Freedom, Hugh Thomas, Eyre &
Spottiswood, London, 1971.

Habana Antigua – Apuntes Historicos, Dr. Manuel Perez
Beato, Havana, 1936.

La Habana Antiga – Apuntes Historicos, Emilio Roig de
Leuchsenring, Havana, 1964

La Aruitectura Cubana del Siglo XIX, J.E. Weiss y Sanchez,
Publicaciones de la Junta Nacional de Arqueologia y
Etnologia, Havana, 1960

Los Monum entos Nacionales de la Republica de Cuba, Emilio
Roig de Leuchsenring, Junta Nacional de Arqeologia y
Etnologia, Havana, 1960

La Ciudad Hispano Americana – El Sueno de Orden,
CEHOPU – MOPU, Caracas & Madrid, 1989

Panorama Historico, Gerlado Castellanos, Ucar y Garcia,
Havana, 1934

Deten el Paso, Caminante . . . La Habana Vieja, Eusebio Leal
Spengler, Havana, 1986

Regresar en El Tiempo, Eusebio Leal Spengler, Havana, 1986

Getting to Know Cuba, Jane McManus, St. Martins Press,
New York, 1989

'The Many Lives of Old Havana', James L. Stanfield, *National
Geographic,* Vol. 176, No 2. August, 1989

Hildebrand's Travel Guide Cuba, Heidi Rann, Peter Geide
Karto – Grafik, Frankfurt, 1985

Cuba – Official Guide, A. Gerald Gravette, Macmillan
Caribbean, London, 1988

Index